The Edge of the Land

The Edge of the Land

The Coastline of New Zealand

Graeme Matthews

Text by Sheila Natusch Wade Doak Jeremy Gibb

Whitcoulls

To Jenny

Whitcoulls Publishers
CHRISTCHURCH   LONDON

First published 1983

© 1983 Graeme Matthews

Whitcoulls Publishers
Christchurch, New Zealand

ISBN 0 7233 0686 9

Designed by Graham Oates

Printed by Dai Nippon Printing Co. (Hong Kong) Ltd, Hong Kong

CONTENTS

'Morning hath broken.' A tui flicks and fidgets about on a coastal flax-stalk, carelessly scattering bright drops of nectar and splashes of song from this summer's repertoire. Later, the tune will be decorated with variations; still later, when flowers have gone to seed and leaves have lost their juicy freshness in the glare of late summer, trees may ring with the monotonous 'chock, chock, chock' from tui throats.

A shag, perched on a guano-whitewashed rock, might for all the world be a sculpture of a shag, until it decides to flump off, very much of the heavier-than-air class.

On another perch, crusted with lichen yellow as egg yolk, sits a piece of Nature's mocking handiwork: weatherworn driftwood, its fluid lines alive with avian rhythm. It is as if the wooden 'shag' is just turning its head to one side, while the real shag seems bent on looking like a piece of driftwood. No wonder folklore abounds with legends of living creatures turned to wood and stone.

The dressing and shaping, grinding and polishing of stone were going on long before the arrival of mankind on this planet, and will, no doubt, see us out. In the meantime, we may well marvel, in all humility, at the shapes and patterns, abstract and representational, achieved without our help; at the time it takes for solid rock to wear down into countless grains of sand, and to be built up again into solid rock—rock that, for all its solidity, will break under the strain of earth movements and the crashing force of the sea. And, as the years roll on, those mighty blocks of stone will be sculptured by wind-blown sand (from other rocks long since crumbled away), smoothed and shaped by slow, solvent rain and salty spray.

Froth and bubble, emblem of evanescence—yet the foam of a receding run of the sea may persist surprisingly long. This briny spume can be picked up and tossed about, by the wind, or by the hands of children, who may remember how the Good Folk use it to make their faery flapjacks. Or is this wild and empty shore some corner of Prospero's enchanted island, where, at any moment, Ariel may enter, invisible, to play and sing?

Sea and sky, sky and sea, wind, tide, currents of air and water—all matter greatly to skipper and pilot alike. The passenger in an aircraft may, if he is not wasting life in contemplation of the paper, glance idly down from his window seat as a lone yacht makes its way across an immensity of brightness crisped and patterned like beaten brass, dazzling to the eyes. From above, the yacht is no more than a black flake, a moth seen for a moment against the light, an episode of the voyage—as, too, is the passing plane to the yachtsman. But those metallic patterns are far from solid and set; there is a rustle and rush of plunging water whose patterns may be clear enough to the airman and albatross, but must be taken as they come by those nearer the water-line. Clouds mass and bank over the land, along the horizon—and there is still a long way to go.

Sheila Natusch

Caring for our Coasts

Wade Doak

As island dwellers we are extremely fortunate: we share borders with no other country; the edge of the sea is our only boundary. Its problems are of our own creation, and in solving them we have a responsibility to the whole planet.

From an early age we are accustomed to making use of the sea for sport and recreation. Few New Zealanders would not cherish rich childhood memories of seaside holidays, tide pool magic, sun and surf, sand and mud. But as our population becomes increasingly urban, there is a danger that we are growing more and more insensitive to the degradation of the coastal environment. It is a sad fact that a new generation of children in our major cities has never seen the sea. Colour television and the backyard pool can never replace the imprint of sea and sky on young minds. If we are to avoid irreparable damage to our coast, there must be a major effort to increase public awareness. We need new ways of thinking about the sea and fresh opportunities for enjoying its treasures.

Ecology, or earth logic, is the pinnacle of all our sciences, giving us the knowledge to operate within natural systems with the efficiency of a business organisation. It has been defined as the science of cataloguing, ordering and inspecting patterns of life —planetary housekeeping. Unfortunately, though, the generation whose scientists discovered the basic concepts of ecology has not yet understood them. Information essential to the survival of the company has not yet reached all the shareholders and fewer of the directors. When this young science is fully assimilated by our society it will be the delight of economists and accountants. Until now they have been denied the chance to examine the debit side of the company's energy transactions and have been unable to manipulate the systems efficiently to maintain

economic stability. The decline of every major fishery and the diminution of our natural resources must be an accountant's nightmare. An escape from this situation is exactly what the new earth science offers; we can now study the whole flow of capital energy through the economic system of a harbour estuary, a native forest or a grass paddock, and then seek to operate that system to maintain steady circulation of the capital flow.

We have now entered the solar age. Fossil fuels will decline in importance as finite deposits are exhausted. The challenge we now face is to recognise the sun as our safest nuclear reactor, and to grasp the fact that, in a solar age, a country's GNP (gross *natural* product) is the measure of the plant material or biomass which its land surface and territorial waters can photosynthesise each year from the energy of our nearest star. The coastal environment is New Zealand's richest province, in this respect, but also the most sensitive to abuse.

First it must be realised that one-third of this planet's surface is earth, that the continental shelves about which we know so little are equal in area to the surface of the moon and that beyond these shelves, the area representing ninety per cent of the world's ocean, is biological desert. The shorelines of the world comprise only one per cent of its surface.

We have to break the habit of treating the open ocean as an infinite resource for a hungry world. For that we would need every tide pool, every mangrove, every piece of shoreline we can spare. In terms of solar age accounting, the daily energy transactions on our coastline make it Wall Street, and the richest areas—sheltered harbours and inlets, estuaries and swamps—are almost twice as valuable, in terms of biomass production, as our best agricultural land, tilled and topdressed by machinery.

Ecologists now see the coastline as a series of habitats which fall into two major categories: those that are sheltered from the wind energy of the open ocean and those exposed to its full force. Modern man threatens each habitat with a special set of problems. We must learn to appreciate these marine worlds and to live within them without causing harm.

As so many life forms rapidly become extinct, we are realising that it is no longer individual species we must protect, but their entire habitats. I was quite astonished to learn, after many years of diving, that the richest marine worlds are the most sheltered parts of our coast. Mud is the basis of it all; the messy places we insist on 'tidying up', the mud flats we reclaim, the inlets we straighten with causeways, the swamps and wetlands we drain for pastures, all the gentlest meeting places of land and sea, are the 'black gold' of tomorrow. In thick, black mud thrive millions of bacteria which readily convert decaying matter into nutrients, a process on land well known to soil technologists.

When a leaf falls the solar energy store it represents usually stays within the forest as leaf litter, but along the shoreline each sea plant releases its nutrients to the tides and beyond. In all the world's oceans, mud and ooze swarm with bacteria. From the upper waters a rain of dead animal and plant life is attacked by them and broken down into nutrient salts and minerals. Over the continental shelves upwelling currents and thermal changes bring these recycled organic chemicals back into contact with sunlight in the upper layers of the sea. Here microscopic plant plankton feed on them, generating a rich algal soup which nourishes the whole marine food chain from animal plankton to sardines and great whales. Such is the im-

portance of algal plankton that it is now believed they are the main source of oxygen in our planet's atmosphere and chiefly responsible for its renewal.

Twice a day, into every sheltered place on the New Zealand coast, a 'tidal topdressing plane' glides in under moon power. Along estuarine shores where wave violence is minimal, over harbour flats where exposure to the sun is seldom fierce, amid grasses, reeds and leafy stalks it flows, bringing fresh food and oxygen to all the low, sly lives that find refuge in that vast surface area. So the crabs and snails, worms and barnacles, shrimps and oysters grow fatter, multiply and release their larvae to the sea. As each tide recedes from all the sheltered havens, fishes gorge themselves on the rich outpourings, wading birds begin to stalk over the refurbished mud flats and on sandbanks cockles and tuatuas close their filter intakes until the next tide.

It has recently been discovered that some two-thirds of our inshore fishes spend part of their lives in estuaries and harbours. Such areas are the most vital life zones on our coast, yet this is where our environmental impact is greatest. We have drastically modified most of our sheltered coastline and severely reduced its productive capacity. With solar age vision we must now reassess this part of our land, viewing it as vital to our GNP, and correcting our mistakes. We must see the reclamation of 'useless' mud flats as an assault on our Fort Knox. The more we reduce the inter-tidal surface area, the less energy we receive; the more we 'tidy up' the shoreline, the less our annual income from the sea.

Harbour management now demands team work, with engineers, hydrologists and ecologists working together. From an ecological survey the various life zones must be established, before any expensive engineering work is planned. Salt marshes, shell banks, mangroves and wetlands perform vital stabilising functions in harbour management. Their destruction increases the need for dredging and, in a vicious circle, spoil is often dumped right on top of these 'stabilisers'. We must adapt our human activities to suit them, to cause minimal disruption. We *do* have a place in it all, we *can* exist with wading birds and crabs, but if we deny them living space, our own survival is the more dubious. For more than sixty million years they have existed without us; there is no evidence that humanity could survive on a sterile planet.

Mention of the word 'coastline' usually suggests rocky shores, sandy beaches, steep cliffs and boulder banks. These are habitats where life forms are especially adapted to harsh physical changes, and we do ourselves harm when we try to impede this process. Human structures on sandspits are a disaster looking for somewhere to happen, and sea walls, heaps of old cars or spoil ramparts are all powerless in this shifting world. We have learnt many a grim lesson around our coast, often succeeding only in making the meeting place of earth and sea more ugly. We must now stop interfering.

From an ecological viewpoint, the richness or biomass of these coastal habitats depends on their stability.

Sand and gravel beaches provide an insecure and shifting environment for a reduced range of life forms. Those adapted to a burrowing existence form very dense populations in such areas—pipis and other bivalves, tube worms and swimming crabs. Further up the shore the sand dunes provide a very fragile habitat in which the least disturbance of plant cover can cause severe erosion. (In Holland access to beaches across sand dunes is now restricted to foot bridges.)

The boulder beach is the harshest life zone of them all. Every storm tosses the big stones around and rubs them together, giving them their clean, close-grained surfaces. Despite the diminished range of organisms in such areas, life is tenacious, and small, fast-moving creatures such as crustaceans manage to find refuge from predators among the boulders and feed on the life-giving currents.

On exposed coasts the greatest threat man poses is pollution. When new subdivisions are bulldozed bare, the sea receives huge volumes of eroded soil. Sewage plants, pulp mills, cement factories and processing industries release thousands of tonnes of particulate matter into rivers and sea, along with detritus from forestry burn-offs and from hill scrapings. All this is a serious form

of marine pollution. For the sea creatures it constitutes a life-inhibiting smog, as tiny gills are clogged, light fails to penetrate coffee-coloured water and solar energy finds no storage cells. Our GNP is diminished and the land is deprived.

A more obvious form of pollution is the release of dangerous chemicals into the coastal environment—pesticide residues, agricultural sprays and toxic industrial wastes—which eventually enter marine food chains. Heavy metals such as lead,

mercury and tin, and chemical compounds such as DDT, dieldrin and PCBs concentrate in the tissues of filter feeders such as oysters, mussels and sea squirts. Those that feed on them further concentrate these substances until those at the top of the food chain—sea birds, large fishes, humans, dolphins and whales—are at risk. Without stricter controls tomorrow's seas may very well swarm with inedible fishes and sea birds may join the moas.

A further threat to the life of exposed shores is over-exploitation. Most of our fisheries work on the assumption that, with increasing industrialisation, we can continue to harvest wild stocks of animals, that we can reap where we have not sown. It is, of course, no surprise that each new fishery quickly reaches a peak in production and then declines steadily. Unfortunately for marine life, market forces by this stage ensure that the reduced production is worth as much as the initial harvest. Scarcity increases the value of each rock lobster, each scallop, each groper steak, until the last one could be worth a day's wages.

Historically New Zealand fishermen have exploited a narrow range of fishes; snapper, blue cod and groper would be our traditional table fishes. But these days their populations have dwindled, and species hitherto commercially neglected are now being fished with giant nets and other techniques geared to an export market.

Our reef fishes, too, are now in the firing line. It may be that in our lifetime these New Zealand fishes will be regarded much as native birds are today. A few more edible species we may farm or raise in sea cages; the rest we will protect, study and enjoy for their grace and colour. It would be unthinkable for a child to bring home a sack of dead tuis and fantails to show his parents, but most of us as children spent afternoons dabbling in the sea for spotties and sprats which we killed without a qualm. Because they live in the sea and we breathe air we have not treated fishes as we do birds, but that is changing now and the edge of the sea is no longer such a barrier. The first humans to breathe underwater went there largely to kill and collect marine life, but new generations of divers are enjoying our undersea world in different ways. Fortunately, the sea is much more resilient than the land and if we restrain our greed, in a decade or so reef fish populations may recover.

It is not, however, just our depredations that affect New Zealand marine life. An ecosystem is such a complex of inter-relationships that any simpli-fication is misleading. Dis-turbances on land have reduced inshore food supplies. Erosion caused by forestry clogs the gills of tube worms on which snapper feed, and estuaries no longer provide the manna that supported big schools of mullet and kahawai. Not only have we caught all the fishes of which our grandfathers boasted, but we have also made it harder for them to feed.

Finning slowly and sinuously like a moki, I thread my way through a golden jungle of kelp plants. Overhead their broad blades writhe and twist on the surface, gathering sunlight and nutrients. Below, like strong hands, their holdfasts grasp the rocks and their rubbery stalks yield easily to my passage. I am very thoughtful about the kelp forest now, since space scientist Jim Lovelock's recent discovery. A specialist in gas chromatography, Lovelock claims* that kelp forests have a role in regulating the atmosphere of our planet which is essential to all mammals and most vertebrates.

Like the thyroid gland, but on a planetary scale, these plants

*Lovelock, J. E., *Gaia—A New Look at Life on Earth*, O.U.P., 1979.

concentrate the iodine in sea water. From the plants it escapes the sea and is blown to the land surfaces to be absorbed by mammals like ourselves. Without iodine the thyroid gland could not produce hormones which regulate metabolic rates and most animals would sicken and die.

A Japanese scientist, Ishida, has shown that a tiny red seaweed that lives on the kelp plants may have a key planetary role in the cycle of sulphur in our atmosphere. Another performs a similar task with the trace element selenium. The sea plants which perform these vital functions exist only in a thin line around the continents and islands of the world and only in the temperate latitudes. Lovelock is extremely concerned at any proposals for the large-scale farming of kelp forests.

If we treat the continental shelves and inshore waters of our planet as badly as we have the land surfaces, we risk interfering with the most vital atmosphere regulators on our planet. New Zealanders have a responsibility for protecting our world which extends beyond these shores.

What then for the future of our New Zealand coastline? In less than two centuries we have transformed these rain-forested islands into an English farm and a North American pine forest. Still we survive, in our cities. But all this bounty came from the sea. If we extend our civilising process beyond the shoreline the future could be very bleak. A mixture of legislation and education would restore us to good terms with the sea and ourselves.

As the basis for a new approach to coastal management I would suggest that we zone our coastline just as we have zoned our cities and countryside. In Queensland the government is creating fisheries habitat reserves. These conservation areas are intended to help compensate the sea for the loss of so much strategic coastline to industrial development. In Europe such areas are called 'marine natural parks'.

As a nucleus for my proposal we already have two kinds of marine reserve in New Zealand. The first, a scientific reserve around Goat Island Marine Laboratory, has been in existence long enough to prove an outstanding success. For many Auckland divers it is the handiest place to see snapper, crayfish and other threatened marine life at very close range. In the newest reserve at the Poor Knights Islands, commercial fishing is banned and there are especially restricted areas where no marine life may be disturbed.

As buffer zones around reserves like these I would propose the setting up of special management areas which I call 'islands of survival'. Areas of great recreational value—usually rocky, greatly indented coastline, or protected harbours in remote areas—are often unsuitable for large-scale commercial operations such as trawling. Within these areas I would suggest that a special management plan be established which would enable local fish populations to maintain healthy levels and would provide a recruitment stock to replenish adjacent, heavily exploited areas. Marine biologists would be consulted to issue a limited number of special fishing licences in these zones, giving priority to charter boat skippers and to local applicants with existing licences.

We are learning the hard way that wild animal populations cannot be exploited at a sustainable high yield as export earners. In marine natural parks fishermen would market catches *only* within the park locality; their licences would entitle them to catch *our* fish for *us*! All New Zealanders would have the opportunity to visit such resort areas and enjoy a wide range of marine delicacies at reasonable (not Tokyo) prices. As in Greece and Portugal, such areas would attract overseas tourists in a world where fresh fish is increasingly rare. We may very well find that we earn more in overseas funds by attracting tourists here to eat our fish than by sending it to them.

As part of a much-needed national programme in environmental education, government-sponsored coastal study centres could be established in each marine park. Now that most New Zealanders are born in cities there is a growing need for opportunities to enjoy a natural environment where human interference has been minimal. Such centres could become more valuable than hospitals and prisons in combating illness and crime, by enabling people to find relief from stress and pathways towards increased well-being. Government sponsorship of such centres could be regarded as a positive move in the area of social and environmental problems, where prevention is much cheaper than seeking a cure. Available to the

of a marked undersea trail which you will later explore with scuba gear.

You can follow up your day's adventure with a film or a reading list at the study centre library. The life style may be simple but the learning aids are superb: dark room facilities, an art studio and a diving school, video cameras and bird watching binoculars, a small film theatre and a group of student guides who live at the centre. Many of them are trained diving instructors and they earn their keep by sharing enthusiasm and knowledge with visitors while completing field work in coastal studies.

With so much to do, your fortnight comes to an end all too suddenly, but there is so much to follow up until your next visit, so many new interests and friends, that life takes on fresh meaning.

Such is my dream. With only three million people and a vast coastline there is for us a challenge and a responsibility. Can New Zealanders give the world a lead? Can we develop an imaginative and creative approach to caring for our coastline, the most threatened and strategic frontier on our planet?

Coastline or wasteline—few projects could offer more reward.

whole community, this would be a new form of tertiary education.

Imagine setting out with your teenage family, youth group, marae or close friends, to spend two weeks at a coastal study centre. You arrive at the verge of an 800-hectare piece of coastal land, with steep hills clad in native bush, sand dunes, coves and cliff-top paths, offshore islands and a clear sea. The whole area is set out with walking trails and vehicle access is carefully restricted. Near the sea coast you enter a village of simple cabins with larger buildings forming a central complex. Facilities are simple, as at a camp or on a marae; you bring your own sleeping bag and queue for meals at a servery hatch.

You are keen to get out on the beach next day because the centre has already sent you leaflets preparing you for a total exploration of the area, above water and below. You may take in some of the push-button tape-slide programmes introducing the forest birds, ferns and lichens, the barnacles and wading birds, Maori pa sites and drift shells. Or, slide by slide, you may watch the unfolding

NEW ZEALAND

SCALE

50   0   50   100   150   200

Kilometres

Three Kings Islands

Spirits Bay   North Cape
Cape Reinga
Cape Maria van Diemen   *Parengarenga Harbour*
Great Exhibition Bay

Doubtless Bay   Cape Karikari

Maunganui

Ahipara Bay   *Bay of Islands*   Cape Brett
Kerikeri
Paihia   Russell
Opua

Hokianga Harbour

Whangarei
Portland   Bream Head
Waipu   Hen & Chickens Is

Little   Port Fitzroy
Barrier I   Great Barrier I

Kaipara Harbour   Kawau I   Cape Colville
Hauraki   Mercury Is
Gulf   Coromandel
Whitianga   *Mercury Bay*

AUCKLAND   Coromandel
Peninsula

Manukau Harbour   Thames

Whangamata

Waikato River   Matakana   *Tauranga Harbour*   Mayor Is   Cape
Mount Maunganui   White I   Runaway
Raglan Harbour   Motiti I   Hicks Bay
HAMILTON   **Tauranga**   Te Kaha   Te Araroa
Kawhia   *Bay of Plenty*   East Cape
NORTH ISLAND   *Kawhia Harbour*   Whakatane   *Waiapu River*

Tirua Point   Tokomaru Bay

Mokau   Tolaga Bay
Mokau River

New Plymouth   **Gisborne**
Poverty Bay

Cape Egmont

Opunake   Wairoa
Manaia   Mahia Peninsula
Hawera
Patea River   Napier   *Hawke Bay*

Wanganui   Cape Kidnappers

Rangitikei River
PALMERSTON NORTH
Cape Farewell   *Manawatu River*   Cape Turnagain
Farewell Spit   Waitarere
Golden   Cape Stephens
Bay   D'Urville I   Kapiti I

Cook   Castlepoint
Kohaihai Bluff   *Marlborough*   Porirua
Sounds   Riversdale Beach
Karamea   *Tasman*   Picton
Bay   Warangi   *Palliser*
Nelson   **WELLINGTON**   *Bay*
Granity   Blenheim   Cape Palliser
Cape Foulwind   Westport   Cape   *Strait*
Buller River   Campbell
Tauranga Bay

Punakaiki   *Clarence River*

Grey River   Kaikoura
Greymouth   Kaikoura Peninsula

Hokitika
Waiau River
Hurunui River
SOUTH ISLAND
Abut Head   *Pegasus Bay*

Okarito   **CHRISTCHURCH**
Lyttelton
Banks
Bruce Bay   Peninsula
Akaroa
Jackson   Haast   *Lake Ellesmere*
Bay   Ashburton
Jackson Head   *Rakaia River*
Canterbury
Awarua Pt   *Rangitata*   *Bight*
River

Milford Sound   Timaru

Bligh Sound   Milford Sound
George Sound   *Waitaki River*
Caswell Sound   Oamaru

Doubtful Sound   Moeraki

Resolution I   Otago Peninsula
sky Sound   Port Chalmers
Chalky Inlet   **DUNEDIN**
Puysegur Point   *Clutha River*
Waiau River   Riverton
Solander I   Invercargill   The Edge of the Land...
Bluff
Foveaux Strait   Ruapuke I
Mason Bay   Halfmoon Bay   *Tautuku Bay*
Curio Bay

Southwest Cape   **STEWART ISLAND**

Drawn by Kelvin Allen
By permission of the Department of Lands and Survey N Z

In the far north, golden sands stretch to Cape Maria van Diemen, with Cape Reinga beyond

Motupia Island, according to local tradition the anchor stone of Maui, stands alone in the Tasman Sea west of Ninety Mile Beach. (Opposite) Snow white silica sands at the entrance to Parengarenga, New Zealand's northernmost harbour

26

A rugged taupata plant grows from bare rock

Sand bar and current patterns within Rangaunu Harbour

Mangrove trees edge the waters of the mighty Hokianga Harbour which, riverlike, extends far inland

The Bay of Islands (above) with Moturua Island in the foreground and Cape Brett in the distance. (Opposite) With water and without—the sunbaked mud flats and warm waters of the far north

Companions by the sea

Constant surf rolling in from the Tasman meets the western coast at Piha

36

Leaving Auckland's Waitemata Harbour, a cruise ship moves cautiously through regatta day yachts, while a boy with his fishing rod finds simple pleasure among the luxury craft in Auckland's Westhaven Marina. (Overleaf) The Auckland Harbour Bridge beyond the estuaries of the North Shore

Auckland's anniversary day regatta on the Waitemata Harbour and (opposite) Westhaven Marina—the great escape from the restrictions of Auckland city life

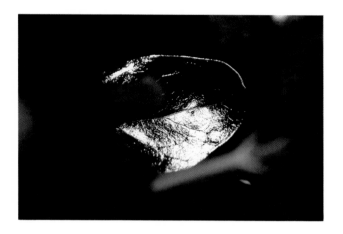

Plant Life on the Coast

The intricacy of a tree in the Bay of Islands. (Above, clockwise from top left) A hebe finds precarious shelter among beach boulders at Southland's Curio Bay, a gleaming ngaio tree leaf on the Kaikoura coast, bright Montbretia *flowers on the Coromandel Peninsula and a glossy taupata leaf at Rarangi, near Blenheim*

Coromandel—driftwood on a beach and (opposite) lush pasture on the Moehau Range flows down to meet the waters of the Hauraki Gulf. Pohutukawa flowers and a lichen-covered rock (opposite below)

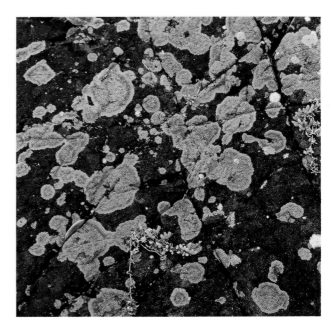

A tiny plant clings to the harsh vertical environment of a seaside rock; the stony Coromandel shoreline of the Hauraki Gulf

White-fronted terns dispute landing rights on a wrecked ship in the Firth of Thames

Using the Coast
(Clockwise from top left) Gathering seaweed washed up after a storm, harvesting salt from the evaporation ponds at Lake Grassmere in Marlborough, collecting pauas at Akaroa Harbour on Banks Peninsula, an oyster farm in Ohiwa Harbour, Bay of Plenty

Tide markings many kilometres inland at Kawhia Harbour; time for contemplation on the shore at Kawhia. Mist-enveloped Motuhora Island (opposite), off the Whakatane Heads, is also known as Whale Island

Recreation on the Coast

Surfing at Raglan, playing ball on Mahia Peninsula, hang-gliding above the beach at Mount Maunganui. (Opposite) Morning fog from the Bay of Plenty rolls in among pohutukawa trees on Waiotahi Beach at Opotiki

Maori horsemen on the sands at East Cape; the driftwood found on these eastern beaches

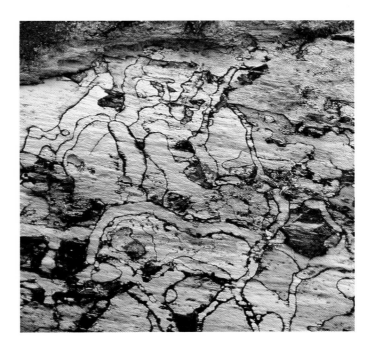

Derelict shipping company buildings at Tokomaru Bay (opposite); the concrete piles of the Tolaga Bay wharf take on an eerie glow in night light. (Above) Tolaga Bay

White-fronted terns; the vast tidal platforms of Mahia Peninsula exposed at low tide

The huge gannet colony at Cape Kidnappers in Hawke Bay is a popular tourist attraction. Visitors can travel along the beach to the nesting sites by tractor

At Cape Kidnappers—towering cliffs on the way to the colony and gannets on Black Reef

Performing dolphins at Napier's Marineland

Multicoloured rock strata on the northern Taranaki coastline

Lighthouses

The Cape Palliser light (above) on the southernmost point of the North Island. (Opposite, clockwise from top left) Cape Palliser lighthouse, changing the bulb in the Cape Campbell light, Nugget Point lighthouse on the south-east coast of the South Island, returning from Stewart Island, the Wairua *heads into Bluff Harbour, the lighthouse at Baring Head*

As uniform as the tides which roll over them—tidal shelves at Castlepoint on the Wairarapa coast; the freighter Pacific Charger *aground on rocks directly below Baring Head lighthouse*

Rocks on the coast

Wellington at night; seen from a hill in the Marlborough Sounds, the interisland ferry heads out into the often turbulent waters of Cook Strait

Ship Cove in Queen Charlotte Sound (opposite) is as tranquil as it must have seemed to Captain Cook during his New Zealand voyages. (Above) The long drowned valley of Kenepuru Sound

Te Mahia Bay, Kenepuru Sound

Animal Life on the Coast

Large-scaled green tree gecko (Naultinus) *(opposite above), tuatara* (Sphenodon punctatus) *and large green cockchafer beetle* (Chlorochiton suturalis)

Nelson's waterfront in the glow of late afternoon sun

Red-billed gulls. (Overleaf) The sheltered waters of Frenchman Bay on the coast of Abel Tasman National Park

A fiery sunrise over Golden Bay means rain to come; groves of nikau palms create a tropical setting on the West Coast north of Karamea

84

A brackish beach pool alongside the Heaphy Track at Karamea; river crossing and beach travel on the Karamea coast section of the track

88

Nikau palms

Port Underwood, with Cook Strait beyond, seen from a high inland hill; the summer-parched country of the Awatere Valley ends in the abruptness of Marlborough's Vernon Bluffs

A double rainbow over Rarangi Beach, Marlborough; Boulder Bank protects calm waters from the ocean—the Vernon Lagoons and the Wairau River outlet are in the foreground

Messing about in boats

Limestone outcrops on the eastern Marlborough coastline

A southerly front moves menacingly up the east coast of the South Island; the Seaward Kaikouras tower parallel to the shore

Bull kelp on the Kaikoura coast

Between the Tides

The lifeless shell of a crab still clings to a rock; a meal too large to swallow leaves its captor cast on the ebb tide; an empty paua shell and a chiton with its armour plated covering are left on the rocky shore

At the beach (opposite); a brief visit to the shore (above) . . . and a longer stay

When the boat comes in at Timaru, the seagulls flock for fish scraps; North Otago's Moeraki Boulders lie on the beach like strange forgotten toys

Stark, stony beaches along the edge of the Canterbury Plains. (Above) A white-fronted tern calls from a seashore rock and a huge rope hawser at the port of Lyttelton provides nesting material for a sparrow

The Pancake Rocks at Punakaiki (opposite) and an aerial view of a mud pattern left at low tide on the Okarito Lagoon in South Westland. (Above) Just out of reach of the waves, this cave was a home for early Maoris, providing valuable shelter in the damp West Coast climate

Low tide—and green algae glows in the morning sun; kotuku—the white heron, a bull fur seal.
(Overleaf) Fishing boats at their moorings in Jacksons Bay on the mountainous South Westland coast

(Above) Man's impact on the West Coast. (Opposite) A South Westland river runs into a calm Tasman Sea after a swift journey from the Southern Alps

Storm-driven waves batter the south coast

Shipwrecks
(Clockwise from top left) Wooden deck remains , Bluff; the minesweeper Hinau *in the Firth of Thames;
the* Amokura, *built in 1889, rusts in St Omer Bay, Kenepuru Sound; a steam boiler at Bluff; former
tea clipper* Edwin Fox *at rest in Queen Charlotte Sound*

The waves of the Tasman Sea touch the shore at the Waiho River mouth in South Westland. Mount Tasman is in the background. (Opposite) Martins Bay, with the vastness of Fiordland lying beyond

116

Fiordland—beyond an alpine tarn a fiord stretches far inland among high mountains; spectacular, glacier-carved Milford Sound

The Geography of the New Zealand Coast

Jeremy Gibb

The coastlines of New Zealand total about 11,000 kilometres in length, about one-third of the Australian coastline, and New Zealand's beaches and coastal landforms are representative of the coastlines of the world. To consider the origin of the present coastlines and their great variety of landforms—spits, barriers, tombolos, deltas, cuspate forelands and so on—we need to go back in time some 18,000 years to when the Last Glaciation was at its peak and a major portion of the sea was locked up as ice. Such was its effect that the global sea level stood some 130 metres below the present-day sea level. The New Zealand coastline lay well seaward of its present position at what is now the outer edge of the continental shelf. At that time New Zealand was one continent except, perhaps, for the Chatham Islands and the active volcano of White Island in the Bay of Plenty. The Hauraki Gulf, Cook Strait and Foveaux Strait as we know them today, did not exist.

From 18,000 until 6,500 years ago the world-wide climate warmed and the massive continental ice sheets melted until only the two ice sheets of Antarctica and Greenland remained. The locked-up sea water was released into the great oceans and the sea level rose at about ten millimetres per year, steadily transgressing the land. Over this period of 11,500 years, the 'great flood' separated the continent of New Zealand into the North Island, South Island and Stewart Island and the many smaller islands now dotted around the coast. Valleys once occupied by rivers and streams were drowned to form the many harbours and tidal inlets around the coast and features such as the Marlborough Sounds. The valley glaciers of Fiordland diminished in response to the climatic warming and the deep U-shaped fiords were progressively flooded by the sea to form Fiordland as we know it today.

The drowned valleys of the Marlborough Sounds

When the 'great flood' ceased about 6,500 years ago at a level the same as that of the ocean today, the coastline was essentially unmodified by coastal processes. Its outline was intricate, with drowned valleys extending inland and ridges extending well seaward. Modification would have been most rapid 6,500 years ago as erosion concentrated on headlands and sediments filled valleys. During the smoothing process, unconsolidated, soft and fissured rocks were trimmed back by the sea into coves and bays, leaving the harder, more massive rocks as headlands. Valleys

These hillsides on the edge of the Wairau Plain were formerly seacliffs

120

were filled with sediment or turned into lakes or partially enclosed inlets by the growth of spits and barrier beaches across their entrances.

Along most coasts, the process of longshore drift (explained further on) was extremely important. Sediment deposited on the shoreline from a variety of land-based and marine-based sources was selectively sorted into various sizes such as sand and gravel and abraded by the action of waves and currents. Coves and bays were successively filled with sediment to become conveyors of longshore drift, allowing the downcoast coves and bays to be filled.

Coastal modification generally slowed as the shoreline approached a smoothly flowing outline and in some places reversals in the general trend took place. Today about fifty-six per cent of the open, exposed New Zealand coastline is static, twenty-five per cent is eroding and nineteen per cent is accreting.

The open, exposed beaches display the full range of textures from fine sand to boulders, including mixtures in various proportions of sand and gravel. Depending on the relative abundance of heavy minerals, such as magnetite, hypersthene, augite and hornblende, compared with light minerals, such as quartz and feldspar, the beaches range in composition from the blue-black ironsand-rich beaches of Taranaki to the pure white quartz-rich ones near Parengarenga Harbour. The gravels may include angular or well-rounded stones of igneous (basalt, andesite, pumice, granite, diorite, etc.), metamorphic (hornfels, schist, quartzite, etc.), carbonate (limestone, marble, etc.), or sedimentary (sandstone, mudstone, conglomerate, etc.) rocks, or mixtures of the four, depending on the proximity of a beach to a particular rock type.

The blue-black ironsands of a Taranaki beach contrast with the pure white quartz beaches of the far north

Between the beaches are either harbours and tidal inlets or rocky promontories flanked, in some cases, by wave-cut shore-platforms. (Gravel beaches are those where the mean grain size is greater than two millimetres and sand beaches are those less than two millimetres.)

About fifty-seven per cent of New Zealand's beaches are sand-dominant and the remainder are gravel-dominant. Both rivers and streams, and eroding seacliffs and shore-platforms supply most, if not all, the gravel. For some

121

coastlines, like the Waitaki and Canterbury along the east coast of the South Island, the rivers and seacliffs supply roughly equal amounts of gravel. For other coastlines, like those adjacent to the Mohaka and Waiapu rivers on the east coast of the North Island, the rivers supply all of the gravel and most of the sand for sixty-five-kilometre and thirty-five-kilometre lengths of beach respectively. Such shorelines are highly sensitive to fluctuations in bed-load outputs from the rivers and could be seriously affected by the construction of hydro-dams which block the supply of sediment to the coast.

Man's mistreatment of his country helps to cause erosion

As well as being supplied from the above sources, sand also comes from the seabed and from long-shore drift in some areas. With the exception of the Taranaki coastline, most of New Zealand's west coast beaches are fed from rivers and longshore drift. In Taranaki, eroding seacliffs make a significant contribution. For the coastlines of

eastern Northland, Auckland and Bay of Plenty and parts of the North Island's east coast, the seabed is thought to be the predominant supply source.

Taranaki seacliffs are being worn away by the sea

When sediment is supplied to the coast from any one of the above land-based sources, it is subjected to the considerable energy of the ocean. The predominant forces in coastal waters are wind-generated waves from the sea. The configuration of the coastline and the nearshore seabed focuses the flow of energy which is responsible for the transport and sorting of sediment through the action of waves and currents. Wave crests usually approach the shore at some angle other than the perpendicular, forming a velocity component parallel to the shoreline. (See Fig. 1.)

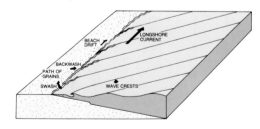

Fig. 1 The processes which result in the movement of sedimentary material

This component is called a *longshore current*, and the movement of sedimentary material caused by it is called *longshore drift*. Similarly, sediment is moved along the beach face when wave swash runs up the beach obliquely and backwash retreats normal to the beach. This movement is called *beach drift*. Taken together, longshore drift and beach drift create a 'river of sediment' moving parallel to the shoreline.

The most important waves that impinge on the shoreline normally originate in storms, reaching the shore either directly as storm waves or, if they have passed out of the area of wave generation, as swell. During heavy storms, waves are steep and extremely erosive. Material from the beach is carried offshore and deposited to form sand bars, where subsequent waves break and expend their energy. Thus further erosion of the beach is inhibited. When the storm has passed, smaller, less steep waves move the offshore bars toward the beach and aid in welding them to the beach face.

There are certain oceanic areas where cyclonic centres are stationary for long periods or follow similar paths each year. Thus the swell reaching any specific coast has a constant direction of approach and is termed the *persistent swell*. The most important generating area for the persistent swell and storm

Swell from the great southern ocean strikes the bottom of the South Island

waves that reach the New Zealand coast is the storm belt between latitudes 40° south and 60° south, known to blue-water mariners as the 'roaring forties', the 'furious fifties' and the 'screaming sixties'. Swells generated in the southern storm belt by winds blowing from any direction between northwest and south all take a general course from the southwest along great circle courses away from the areas of generation.

The persistent southerly swell generated in the southern storm belt determines the regional pattern of net drift around all but the protected parts of the New Zealand coastline. For the protected parts, the pattern of net drift is local and may be determined either by refraction of the persistent southerly swell, or by wind-waves and swells from the northerly quadrant. (See Fig. 2.)

With the exception of the Northland-Auckland peninsula, the islands of New Zealand lie approximately southwest and northeast. Hence a strong *net northward longshore drift*, set up by the persistent southerly swell, occurs along exposed parts of the east and west coasts. The west coast of the Northland-Auckland peninsula sweeps around to the northwest so that the refracted southerly swell is nearly normal to this coast. In this situation the longshore component is reduced so that more material is brought into the area than moves out, resulting in accretion. The well-known long, sandy beaches and dunes of the Manukau barrier, Kaipara barriers and Aupouri tombolo in the far north are evidence of this.

Parts of the New Zealand coastline are protected from the persistent southerly swell. Along the South Island's east coast, Otago, Banks and Kaikoura peninsulas protect Blueskin Bay, Pegasus Bay and North Beach respectively. Golden Bay and Tasman Bay are protected from the

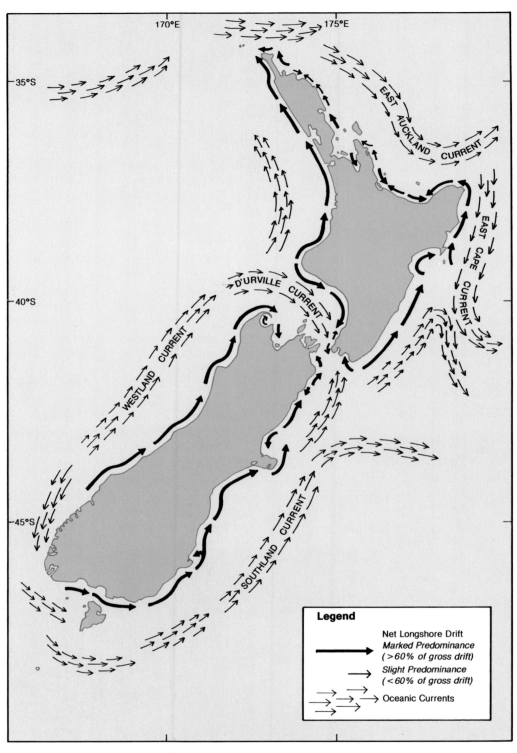

Fig. 2 This sketch map shows the direction of net longshore drift around the coastline of New Zealand

south by the South Island, with Farewell Spit providing shelter from the west for Golden Bay. Between Cape Runaway and North Cape, the North Island protects the coastlines of the Bay of Plenty, Hauraki Gulf and eastern Northland from the south. The 'protected' coastlines are exposed to wind-waves and swells from the northerly quadrant and the direction of drift is *counter* or *oscillatory*.

As a general principle, on a

The influence of the southerly swell is felt as far north as Ninety Mile Beach

New Zealand coasts. Along the west coast of the North Island, the blue-black ironsand-rich beaches of Taranaki grade progressively northwards to the light-yellow fine sands of Ninety Mile Beach. When one looks at the minerals in the sands, one finds a decrease northwards in the heavy ironsand mineral titanomagnetite, and a corresponding increase in the light minerals, quartz and feldspar. The predominant source of the ironsand is the andesite rocks and volcanic ashes of the Egmont volcanic region.

South of Cape Egmont the beaches also become lighter in colour and there is a corresponding decrease in the percentages of heavy minerals. Unlike the light-yellow beaches of Northland, the fine sandy beaches of western Wellington are light grey due to the presence of fine greywacke-derived particles that have been transported

coastline dominated by longshore drift, small particles tend to outrun larger particles as do light, less dense minerals compared to dense, heavy minerals. There are many examples of this fundamental principle to be seen around the

Quiet now, Mount Egmont still affects the composition of the North Island's west coast

to the coast by rivers such as the Rangitikei, Manawatu and Otaki that drain the Ruahine and Tararua ranges.

The process of longshore drift is responsible not only for selectively sorting and abrading the beach sediments, but also for the formation of coastal landforms such as spits, barriers, tombolos and cuspate forelands. Excellent examples of spits are Farewell Spit and the Nelson and Wairau boulder banks. Farewell Spit is the final resting place for the net northerly drift of sand along the South Island's west coast, the Nelson boulder bank is formed from igneous gravels derived from the eroding seacliffs at McKays Bluff and the Wairau boulder bank from Awatere River-derived gravels.

The boulder bank at the Vernon Lagoons in Marlborough has been built up from deposited sediment

The developing cuspate foreland at Paraparaumu on Wellington's west coast is forming in the 'wave-shadow' created by Kapiti Island which acts as a giant offshore breakwater, reducing wave energy from the prevailing northwest waves. Longshore currents lose velocity as a consequence of this effect and deposit most of their load to form the cusp. The growth of this landform is causing adjustments in the position of the shoreline and is one of the main causes of the serious coastal erosion at Raumati and Paekakariki to the south. Should the cuspate foreland continue growing it will eventually weld on to Kapiti Island and a tombolo or peninsula will be formed similar to the Aupouri tombolo in the far north welded to the volcanic rocks of North Cape. A tombolo is unlikely to form at Paraparaumu, however, because of the fierce tidal currents scouring sand in the Rauoterangi Channel between Kapiti and the mainland.

The rocks forming the seacliffs, promontories and shore-platforms that separate the beaches around New Zealand vary in hardness and strength so that their erosion susceptibility ranges from extreme to very low. For example, in the East Cape region, the extensively deformed and disrupted sandstone-siltstone rocks are extremely susceptible to landsliding and are eroding up to one metre per year. As the sea keeps undermining the cliffs they continue to slide into the sea. By contrast, in the same area the very hard and massive volcanic rocks between Matakaoa Point and Cape Runaway are essentially static and are not susceptible to landslides.

Wave-cut shore-platforms fringing eroding seacliffs are prominent coastal landforms along the east coast of New Zealand. As the cliffs are worn back, a wave-cut platform is left in front, sloping gently seaward to mark the lower level at which waves effectively erode. As the cliff recedes, the shore-platform grows in area and an increasing proportion of the available wave energy is expended in transporting sediment across its surface and, inevitably, the rate of

A wave-cut shore-platform on the Kaikoura Peninsula

cliff recession decreases.

There may be patches of sand and gravel in depressions, and fringing beaches strewn with fallen debris along the toe of the cliffs, but all such material is continually being broken up by the waves and used by them for further erosive work, until finally it is ground down to sizes that can be carried away by currents. The platform itself is abraded by the sweeping of sand and gravel to and fro across its surface. On many platforms, erosion-resistant strata form ramparts which are higher in elevation than the platform surface, but are generally covered at high tide.

In New Zealand, the shorelines of greatest economic investment are generally the many diverse and pleasant sandy beaches. Catch phrases such as a 'view of the sea' or a 'short stroll to the water's edge' have lured the public into extending residential development into hazardous areas next to the beach. The effect has been disastrous and houses have either been lost or threatened at beach-front settlements along Wellington's west coast, Wainui Beach at Gisborne, Ohiwa Spit in the Bay of Plenty and along the east coast bays of Auckland, to name but a few.

Combating any particular coastal hazard is usually very expensive; present-day costs for coastal protection works such as sea-walls, groynes and breakwaters range from $150 to $2,000 per linear metre of coastline in New Zealand. In the case of urban development, such costs can be avoided simply by the provision and management of an adequate width of land, or *coastal hazard zone*, between the development and the beach.

Coastal railway protection works in the South Island

How appropriate is that old saying, 'prevention is better than cure'. In the long run, learning to live with nature is the best way to live. When one strolls along the beach and perhaps experiences that 'oceanic feeling' of peace and relaxation, one should never forget that our New Zealand coastline is especially at the mercy of the ever-changing and tempestuous forces of nature.

Seeking relief from the confines of the bush, a group of red deer cavort in the surf on a remote Stewart Island beach